KANDY MAGAZINE

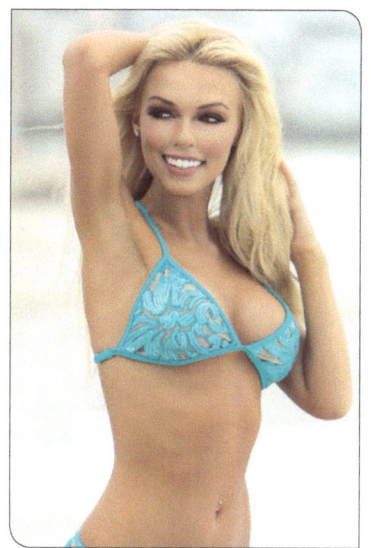

Cover Model:
Trashell Thompson

Photo:
Mike Prado

Hair & Makeup:
Susana Betancourt

INSIDE

FRONT & BACK

COVERS

LEFT BLANK

INTENTIONALLY

<--------------

<--------------

Letter from the EDITOR

Ah February! The dead of winter. What better way to warm up our fellow Kandy readers than with a swimsuit issue. This year we feature the ladies of Tropic Beauty. These photos were taken in Miami Los Angeles, and Las Vegas.

We flew Miss Tropic Beauty Trashell Thompson of Atlanta, Georgia to Miami Beach for her Kandy magazine cover shoot where she met up with Kandy photo director Mike Prado. The weather was less than cooperative for her two day shoot but Trashell and Mike still were able to create magic.

Next up was Miss Photographic Lauren Smith photographed in Los Angeles. Once again, Kandy photo director Mike Prado was up for the task. This time set in the Hollywood Hills, with a pool overlooking the former residence of Britney Spears, Lauren made a hot day a whole lot hotter.

Last, but not least, were Trashell's and Lauren's fellow top 10 Tropic Beauties photographed in sin city Las Vegas. Casey Boonstra of Australia was first runner-up and she was joined in the top 5 by Kandy girl Ednyr Marie of Orlando, Caitlyn of Atlanta, and Jennifer of NYC.

Rounding out the top 10 were Kandy girls Alessandra Sironi and Shelby James, Miss Photogenic Lauren Smith, Mariah of San Diego, and Stella of Australia. Congratulations to all the ladies and all the competitors who made the world finals in Las Vegas.

Kandy will be back later this month with a full, regular issue featuring your favorite sports opinions, auto and gadget reviews, fashion and style advice, sex and dating tips from the Kandy girls as well as a plethora of entertainment content.

Until then,

Cheers!

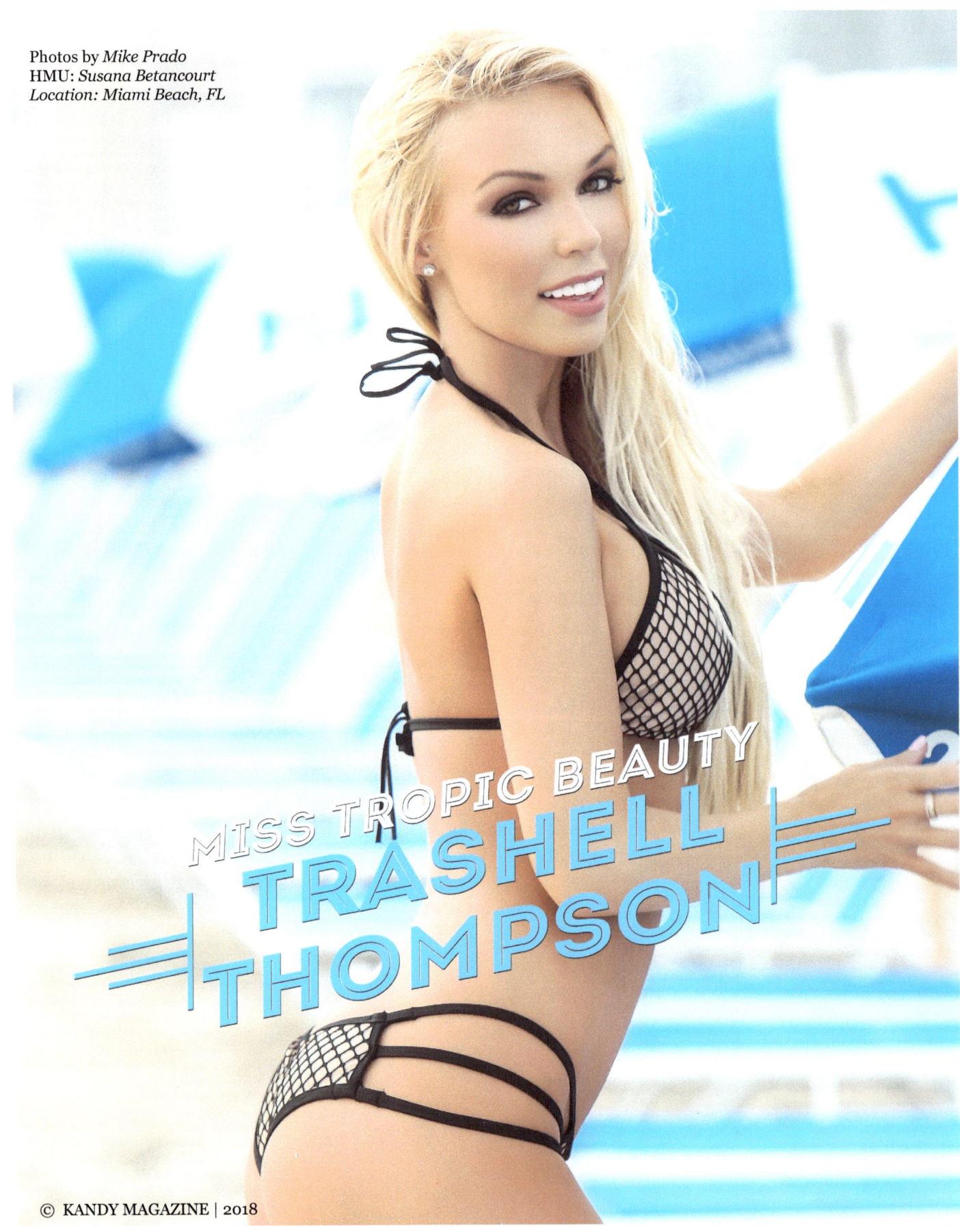

MISS TROPIC BEAUTY
Trashell Thompson
Interview by Ron Kuchler

When Tropic Beauty assembled more than 80 of their local, regional, and international pageant winners in Las Vegas it brought out a crowd of celebrity judges including yours truly. Never one to shy away from a challenge of finding the best of the best it was a monumental task to crown Miss Tropic Beauty. It was good to see the judges concurred with this one judges choice for Miss Tropic Beauty, Trashell Thompson.

What do you love most about TB?

Tropic beauty has been one of the best experiences that I have ever had in the industry. The Tropic Beauty brand cultivates a competitive energy but with integrity and positivity. The relationships that I have built with other Tropic Beauty models have been the highlight of my experience. I have made long lasting friendships with women from all over the world and we constantly build each other up and have formed a bond or a sisterhood as a result of our time with TB.

How many years have you been to nationals?

I've had the pleasure of being invited to nationals for five years.

How did you get involved in TB?

It was really on a whim! One of my friends in Atlanta had entered a local bikini contest at Opera Nightclub. She encouraged me to enter as well. The rest is history. I won that contest and was invited to the nationals in Las Vegas as a result.

We were on hand for the finals in Vegas and there were some amazing personalities on hand as judges. Did you get a chance to chat with Robin Leach?

Unfortunately, I did not get a chance to chat with Mr. Leach. I would've liked to as I am a fan of his show.

What keeps you busy outside of representing Tropic Beauty?

I enjoy staying active and as a result my interests are vast and varied. You are just as likely to find me four-wheeling or riding horses as you would be modeling swimsuits for a local designer at the W hotel. I enjoy traveling to new places with my friends and taking care of my pups, Shuba and Bleu. I recently have challenged myself to become a licensed real estate agent in Atlanta. I have always enjoyed new projects and challenges and I think it's very important for women to surround themselves with good friends and people who encourage them to achieve their dreams. I also mentor other young women who are thinking about getting into the industry (modeling) and Tropic Beauty.

What do you love most about Georgia?

I'm a Georgia girl, born and raised. To me, this is home. My family and friends are here, and I love what being here offers me. Atlanta is a great city to live in and I've met people from all areas of the country. We aren't too far from some of the best beaches in the world - and I've been to many beaches. We have mountains, countryside, and islands. We have sports galore, and I love going to Braves and Falcons games. We have our new soccer team and offers some of the best shopping in the southeast. There's never a lack of things to do. Georgia is the heartbeat of the South.

We flew in from southern California. You flew down from Atlanta. We meet in Miami for a two-day shoot in early August. And yet we run into challenges. What did you love most and share with the readers one of the unexpected challenges.

The Kandy shoot was so much fun! We shot in a really amazing hotel in Miami and the photographer made me feel very comfortable! The day was great, but if I could have changed anything, the weather gods were not cooperating with what we were trying to do.

KANDY COVER MODEL

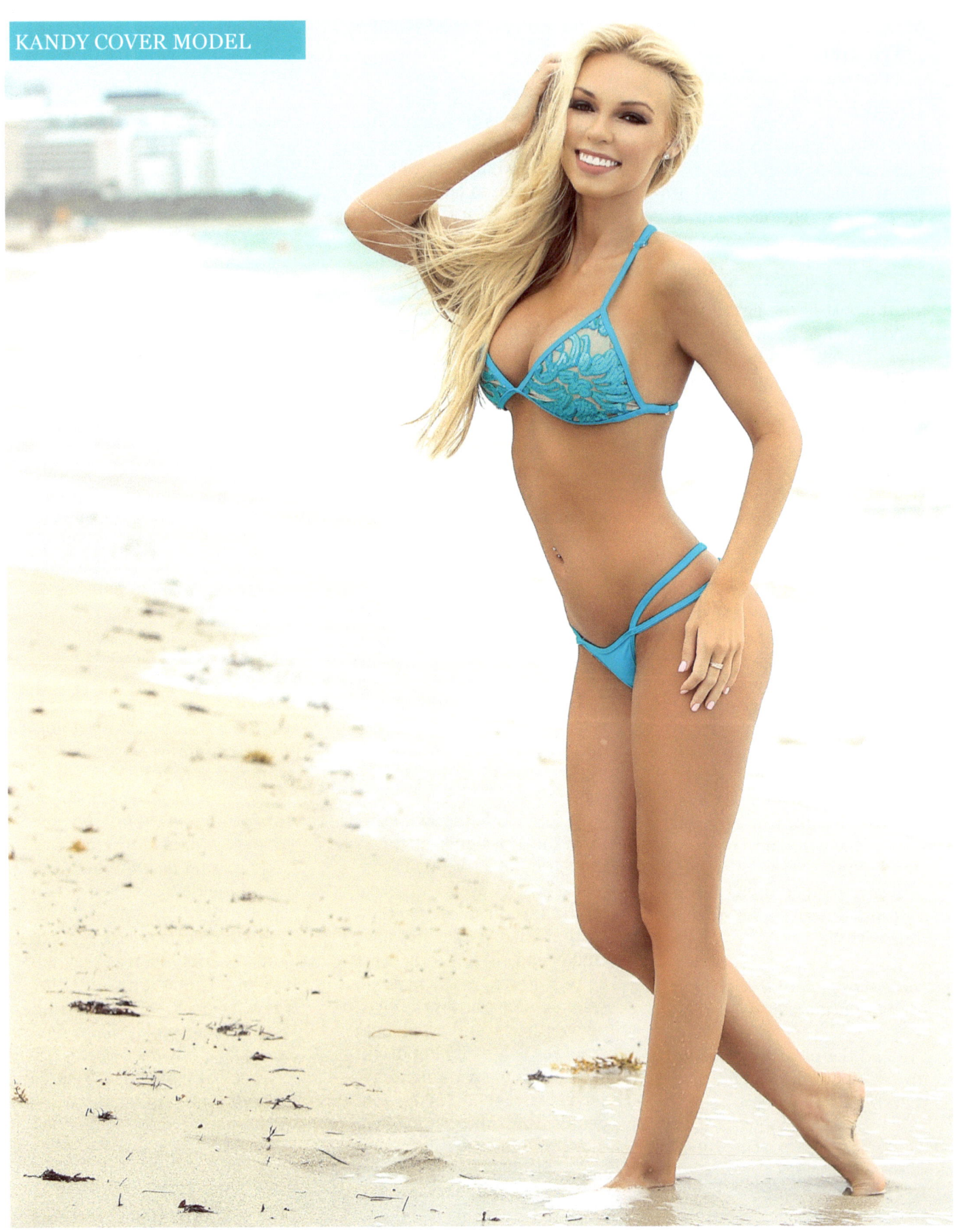

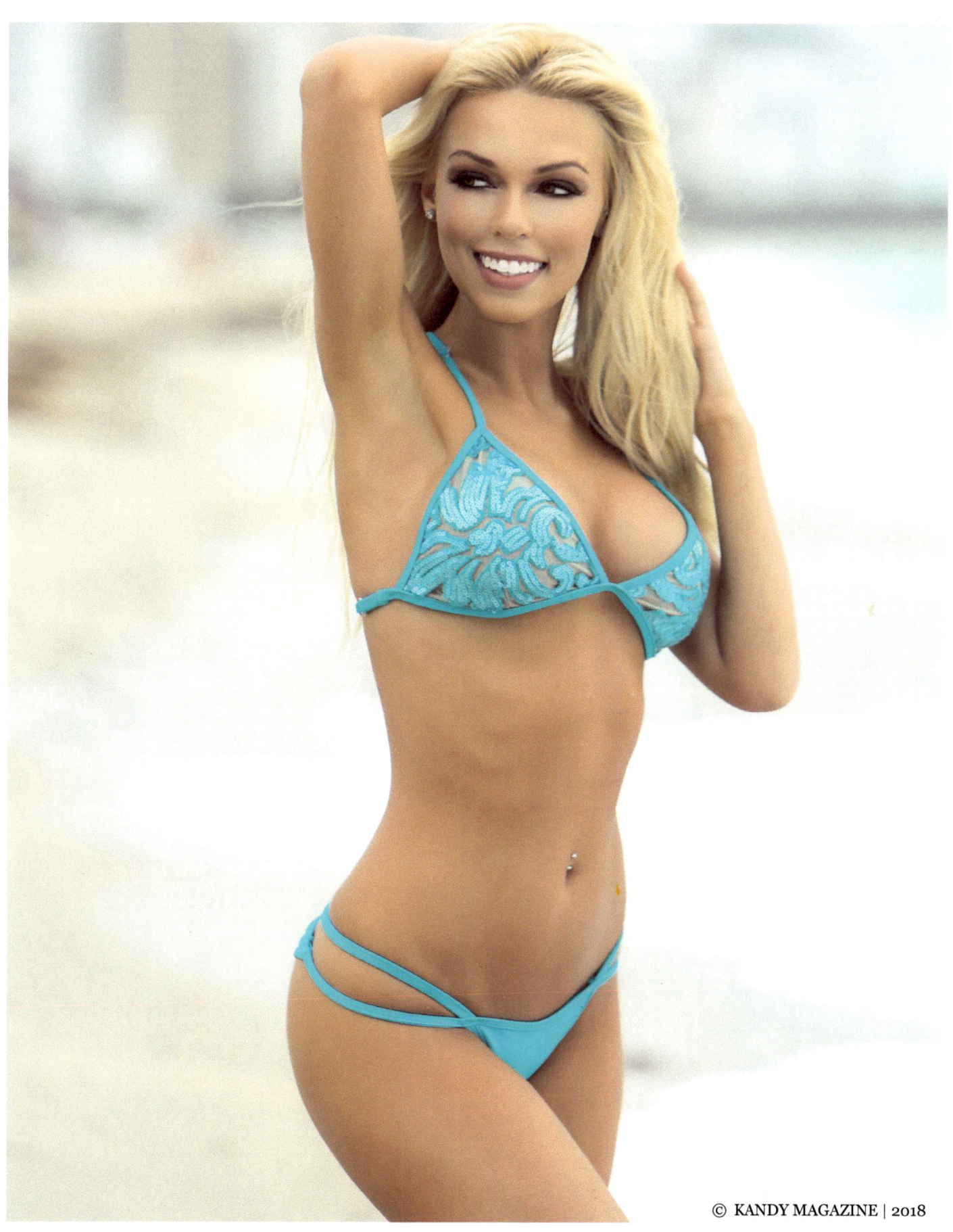

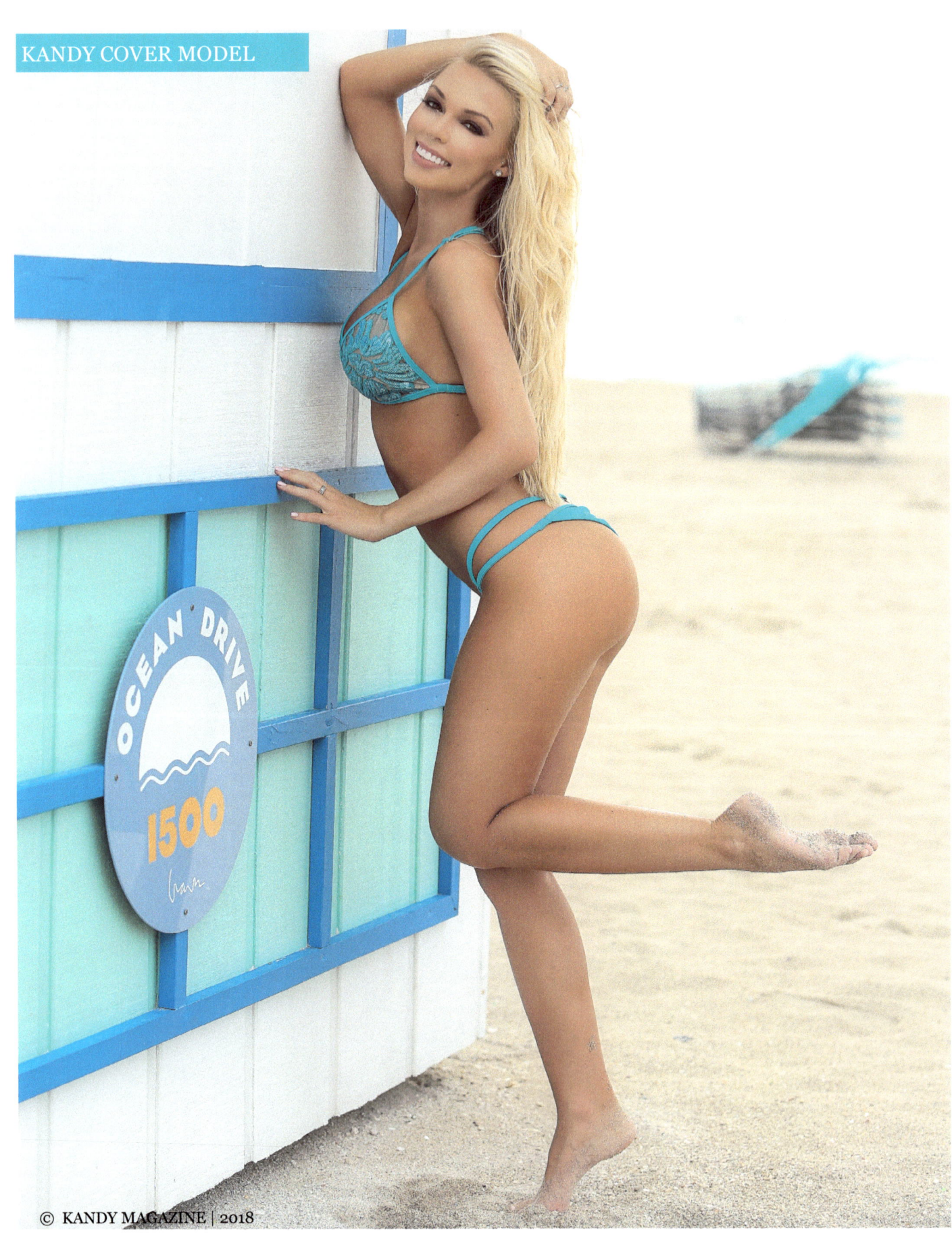

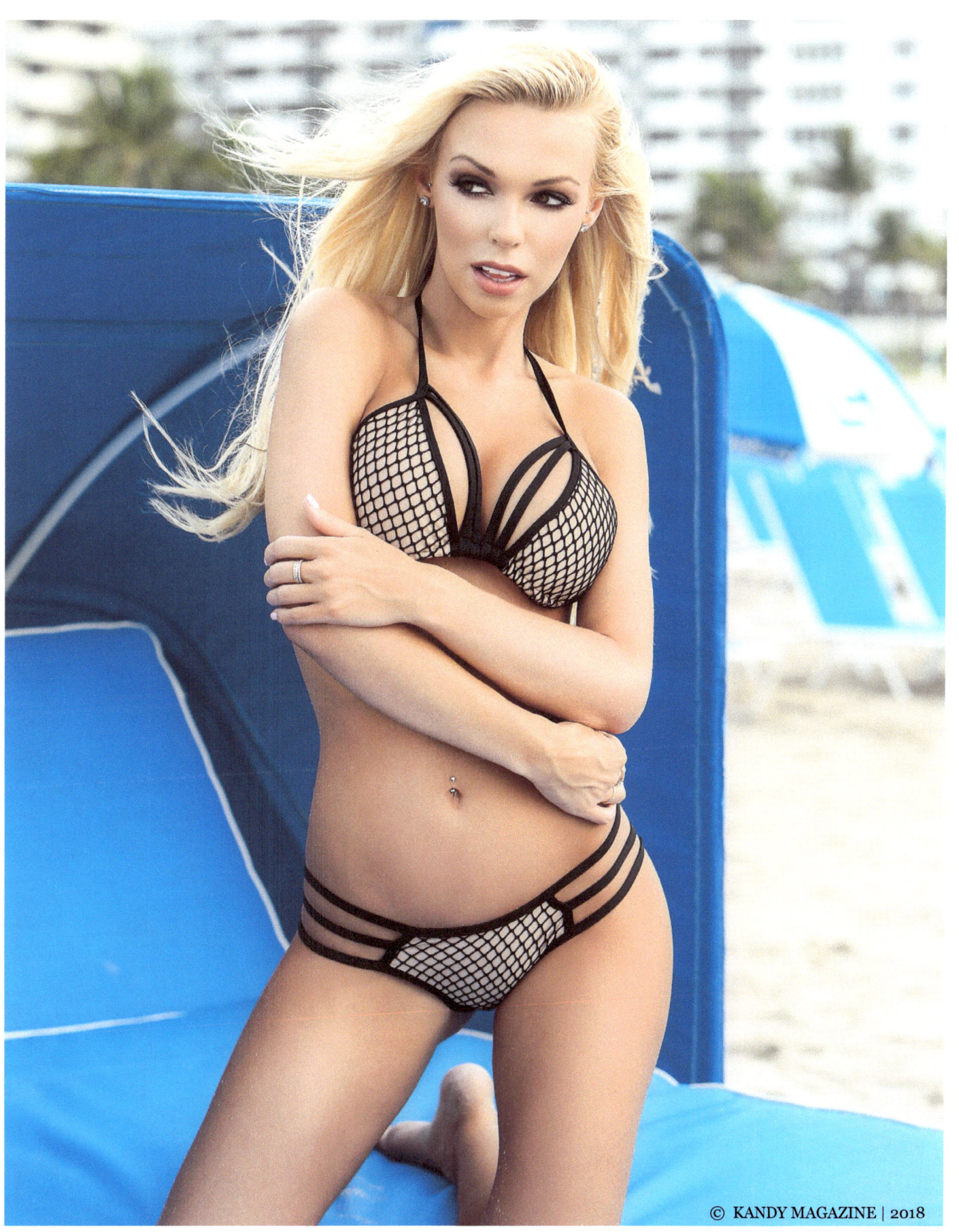

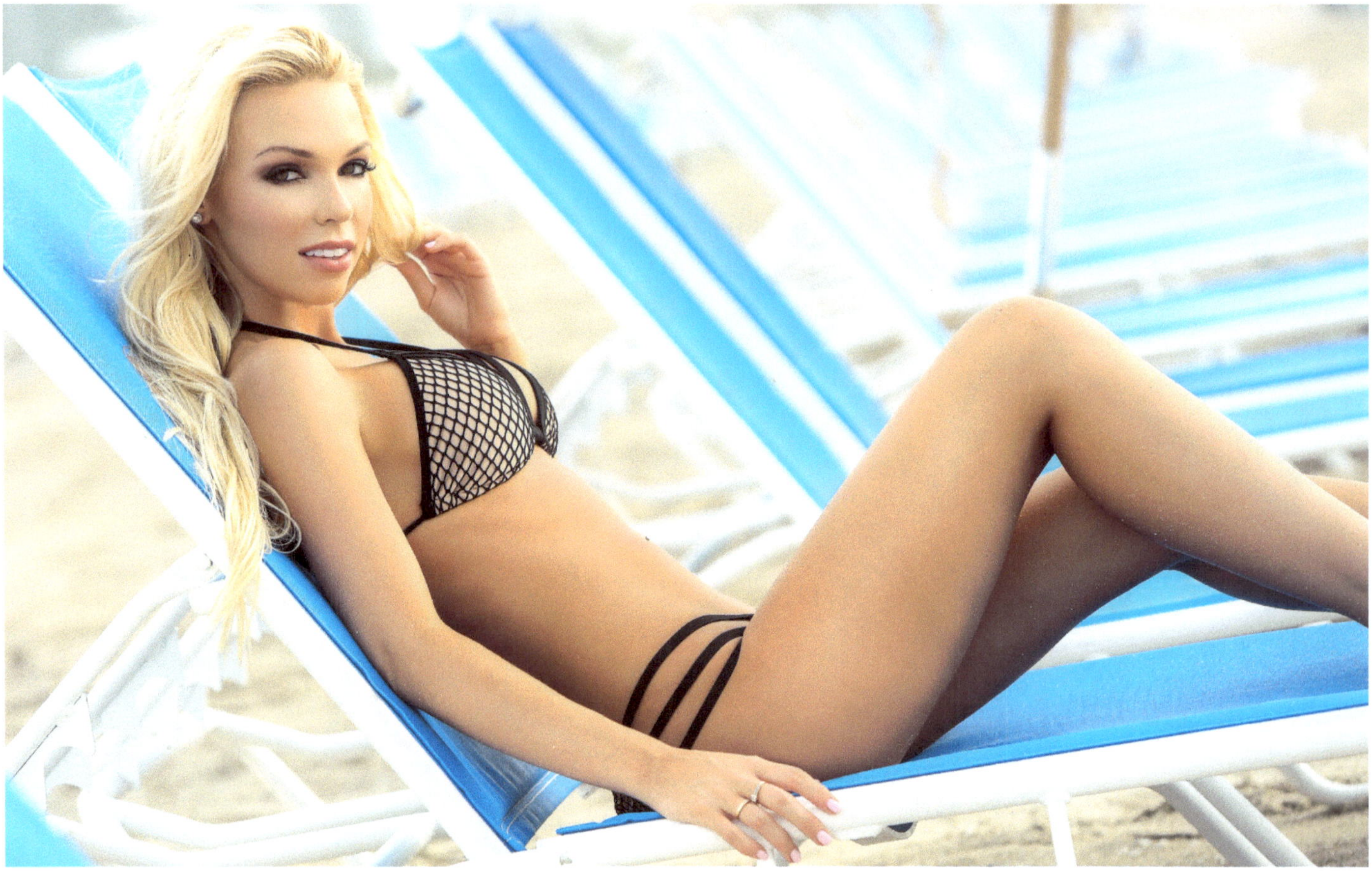

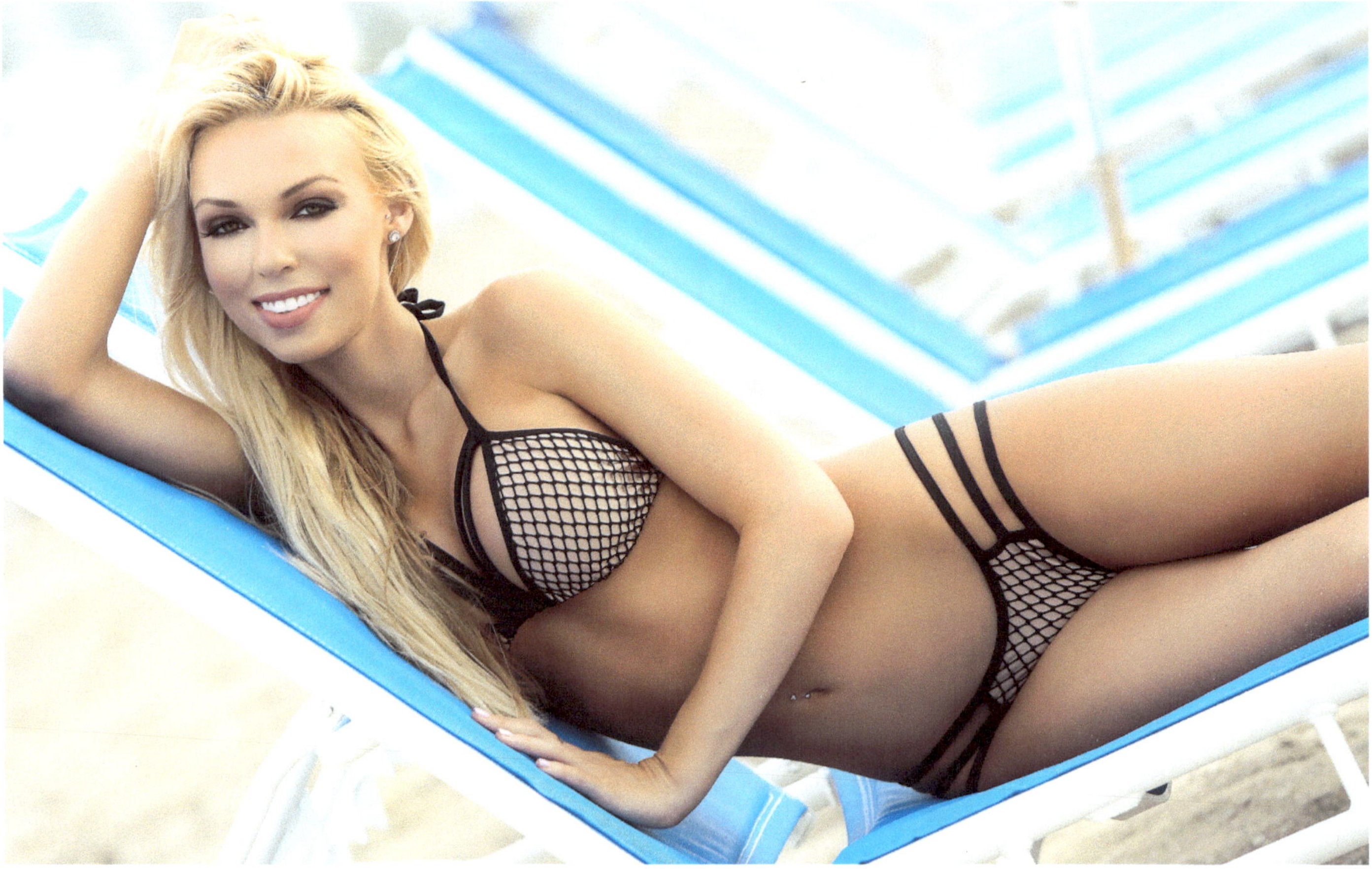

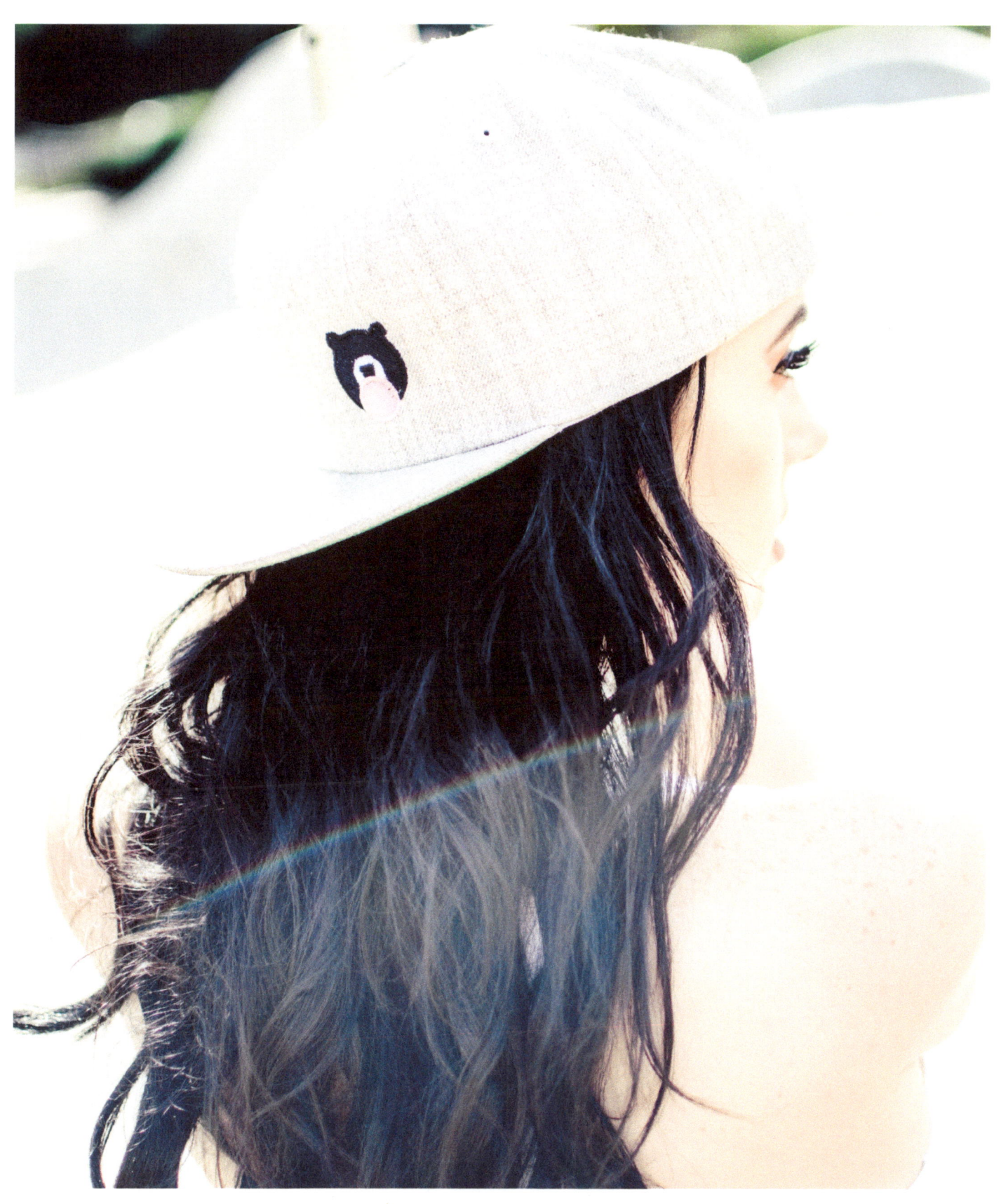

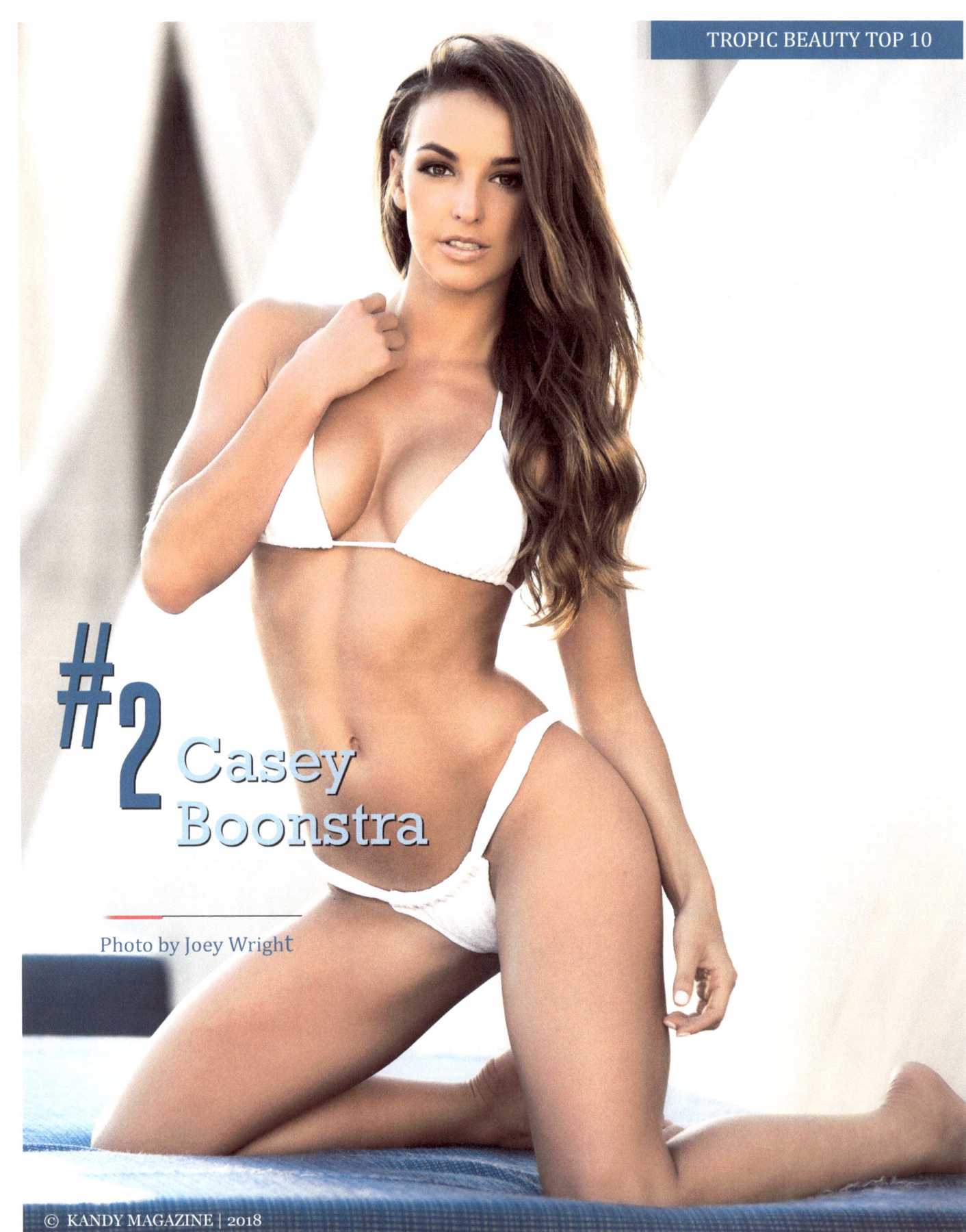

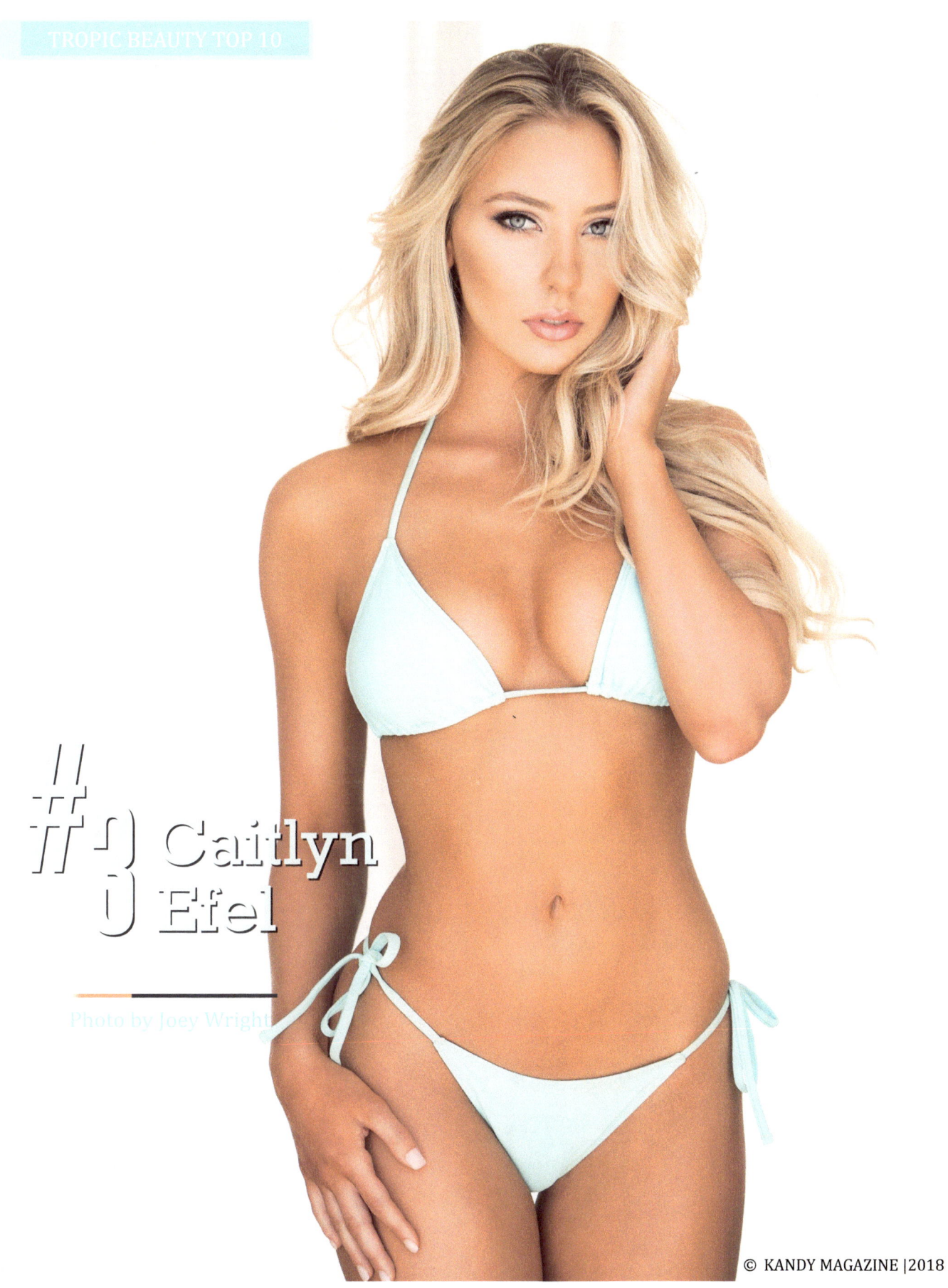

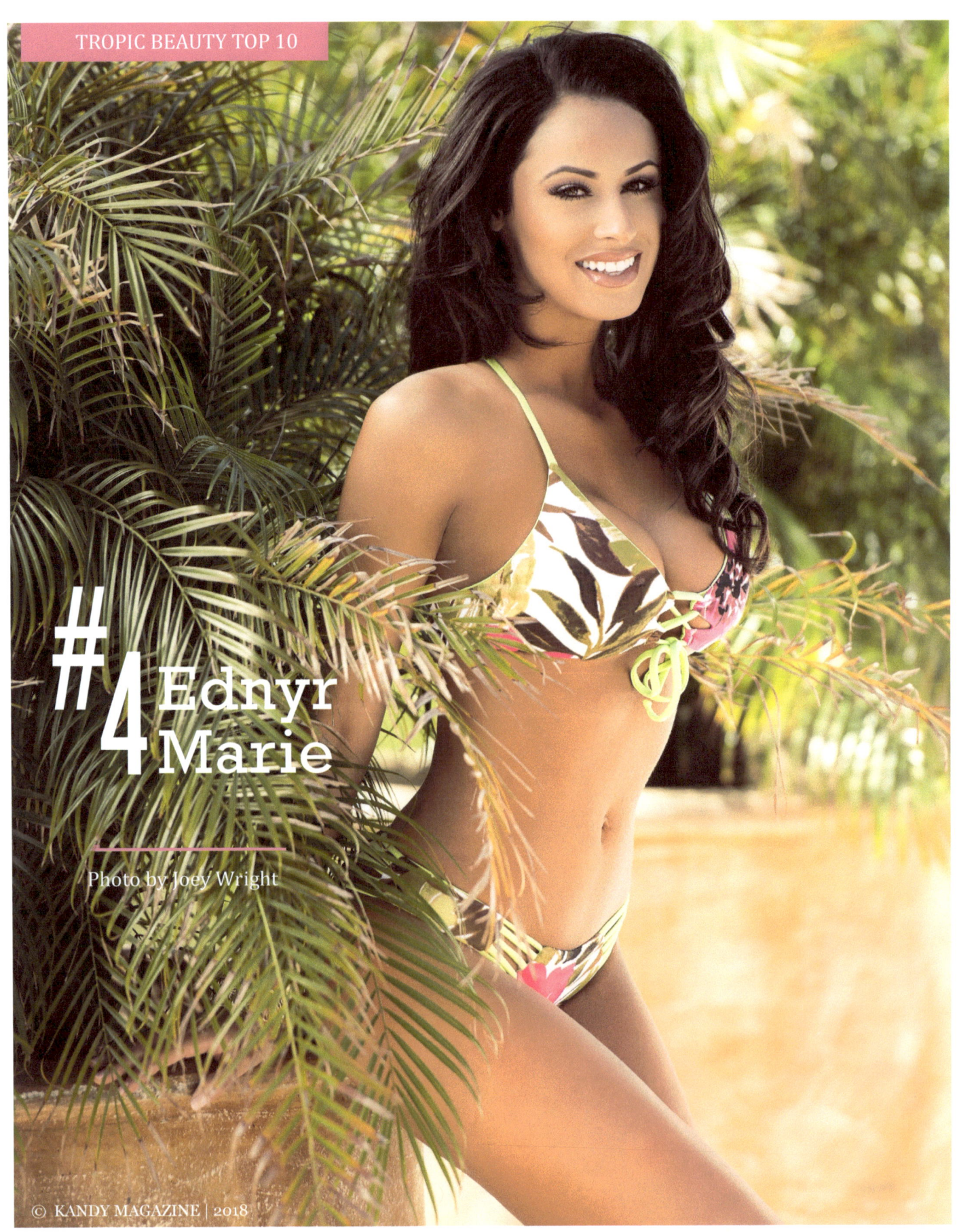

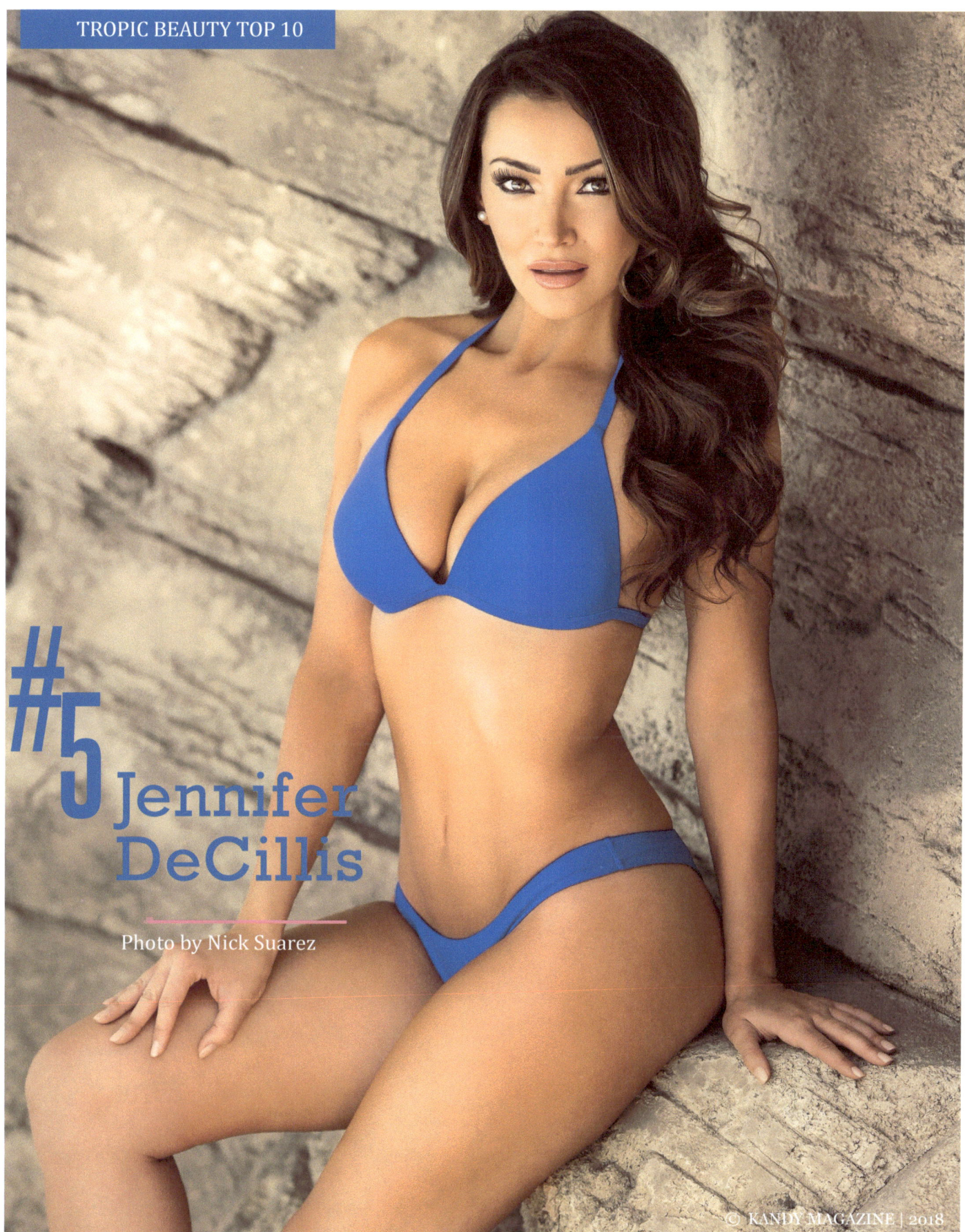

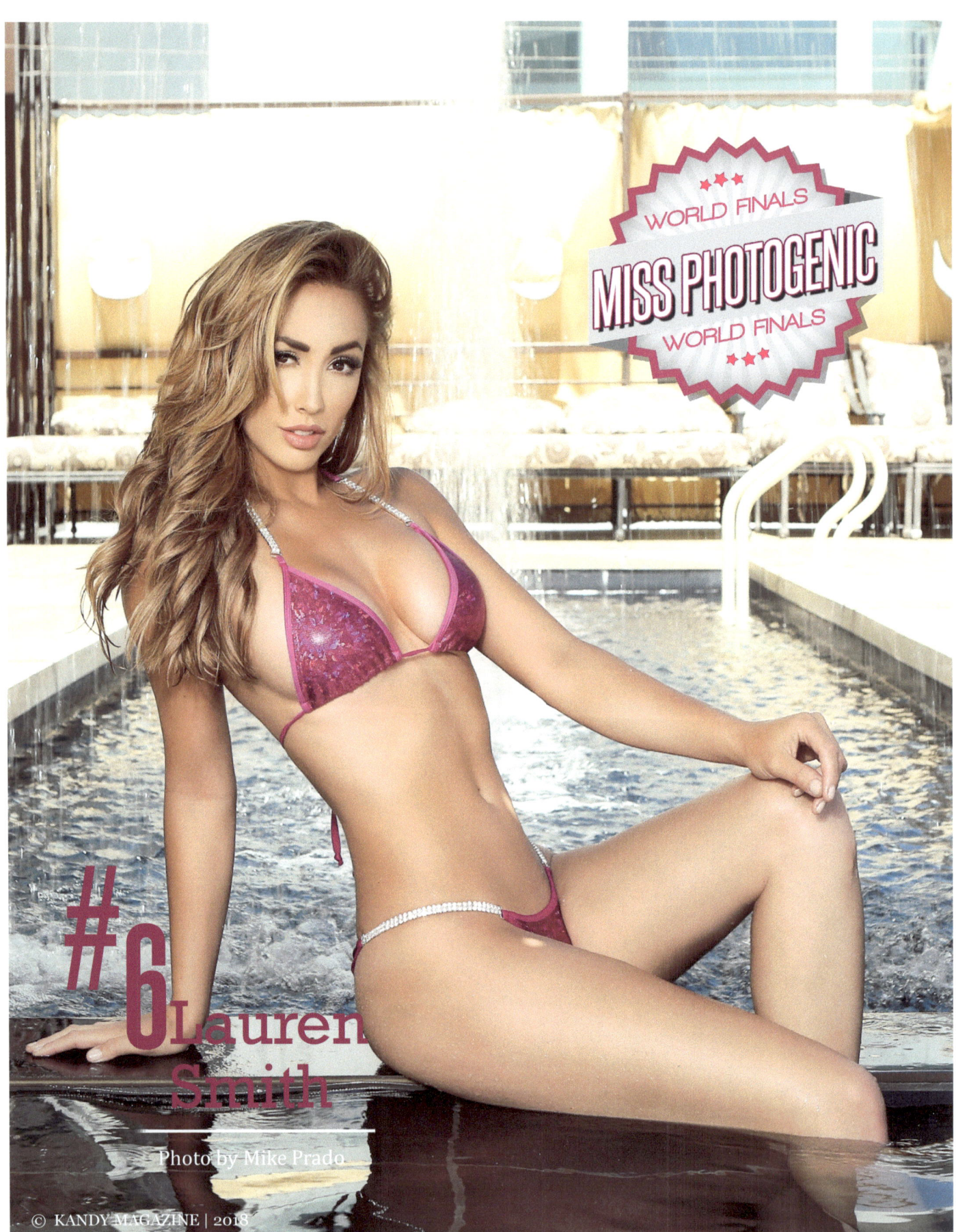

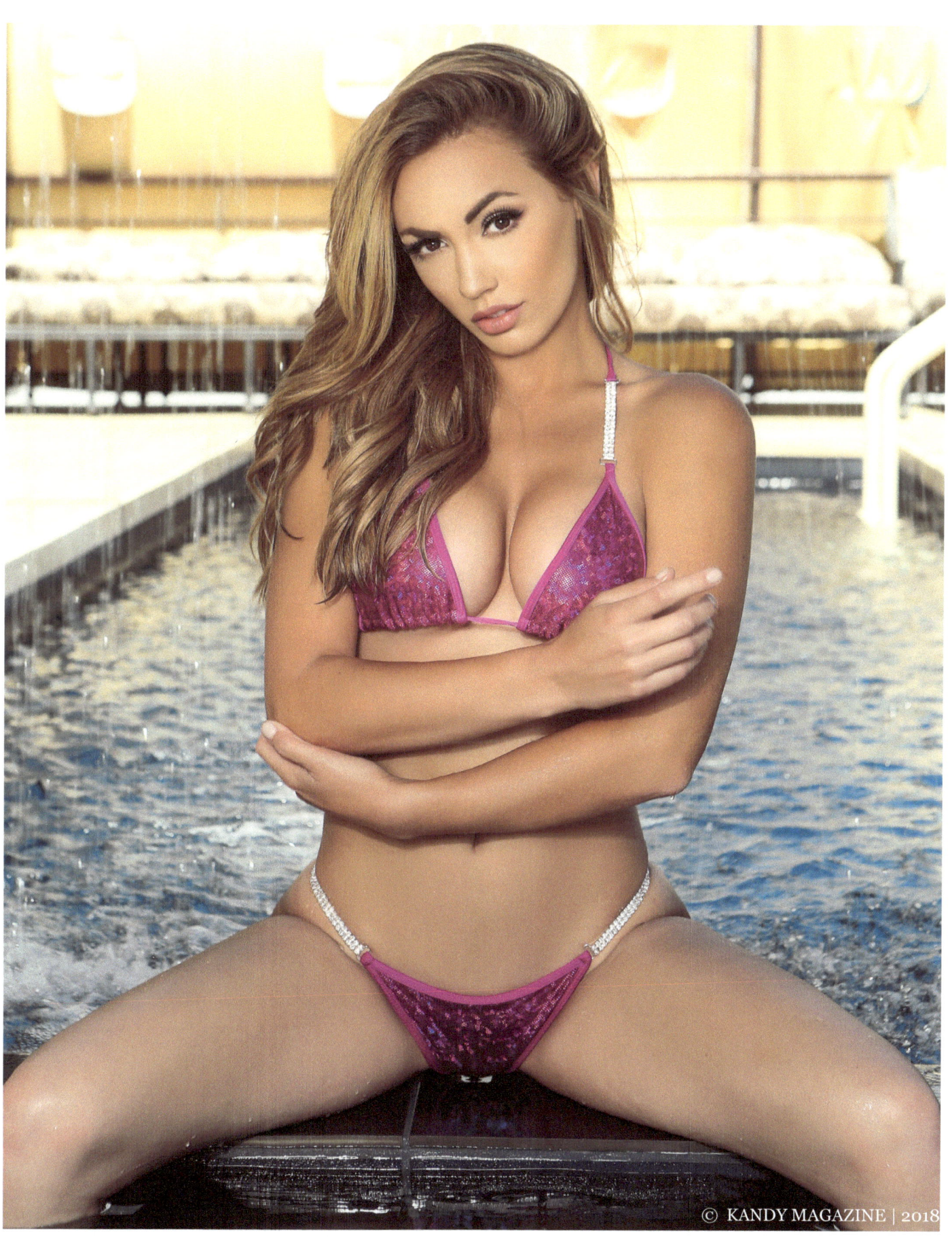

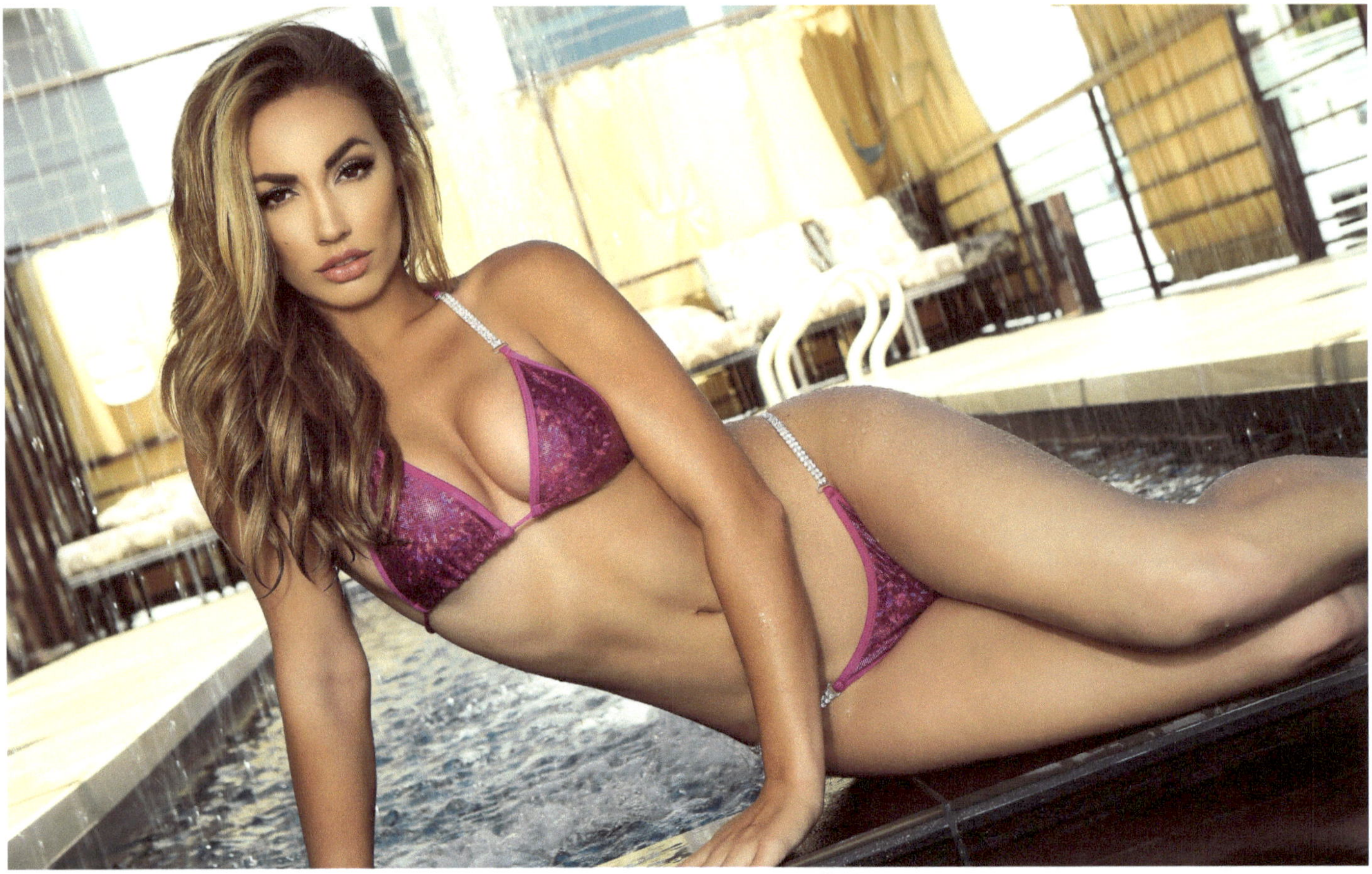

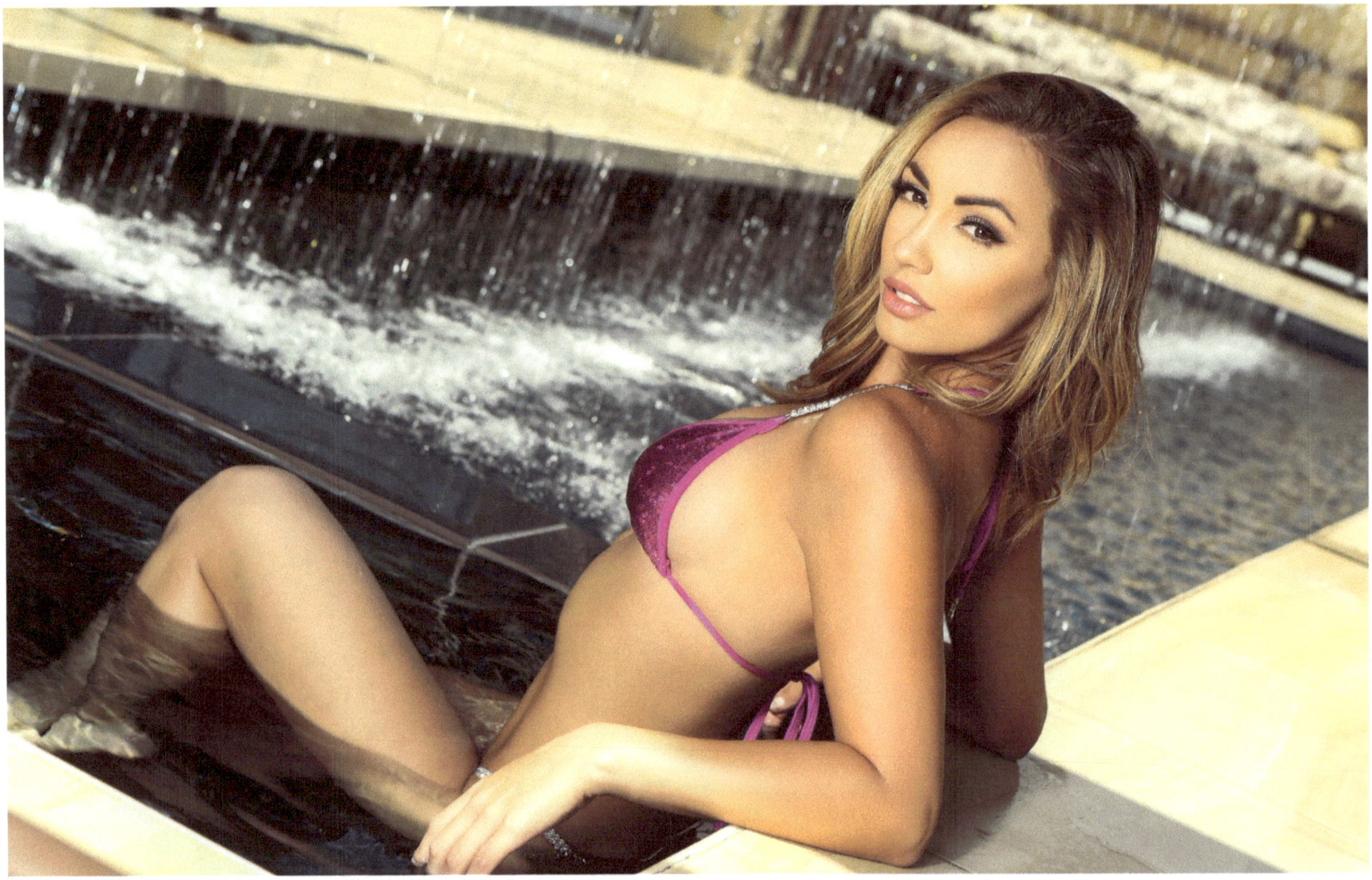

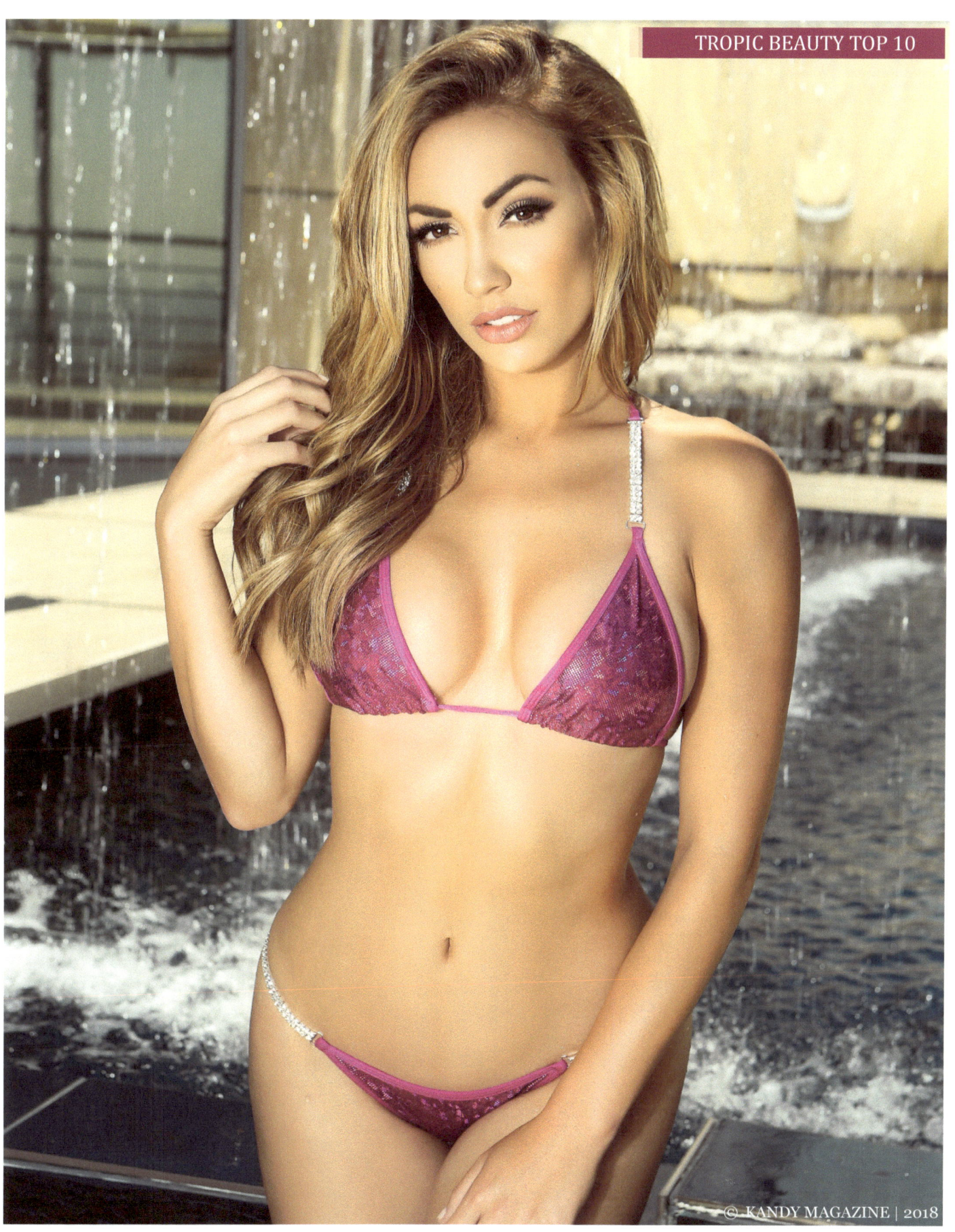

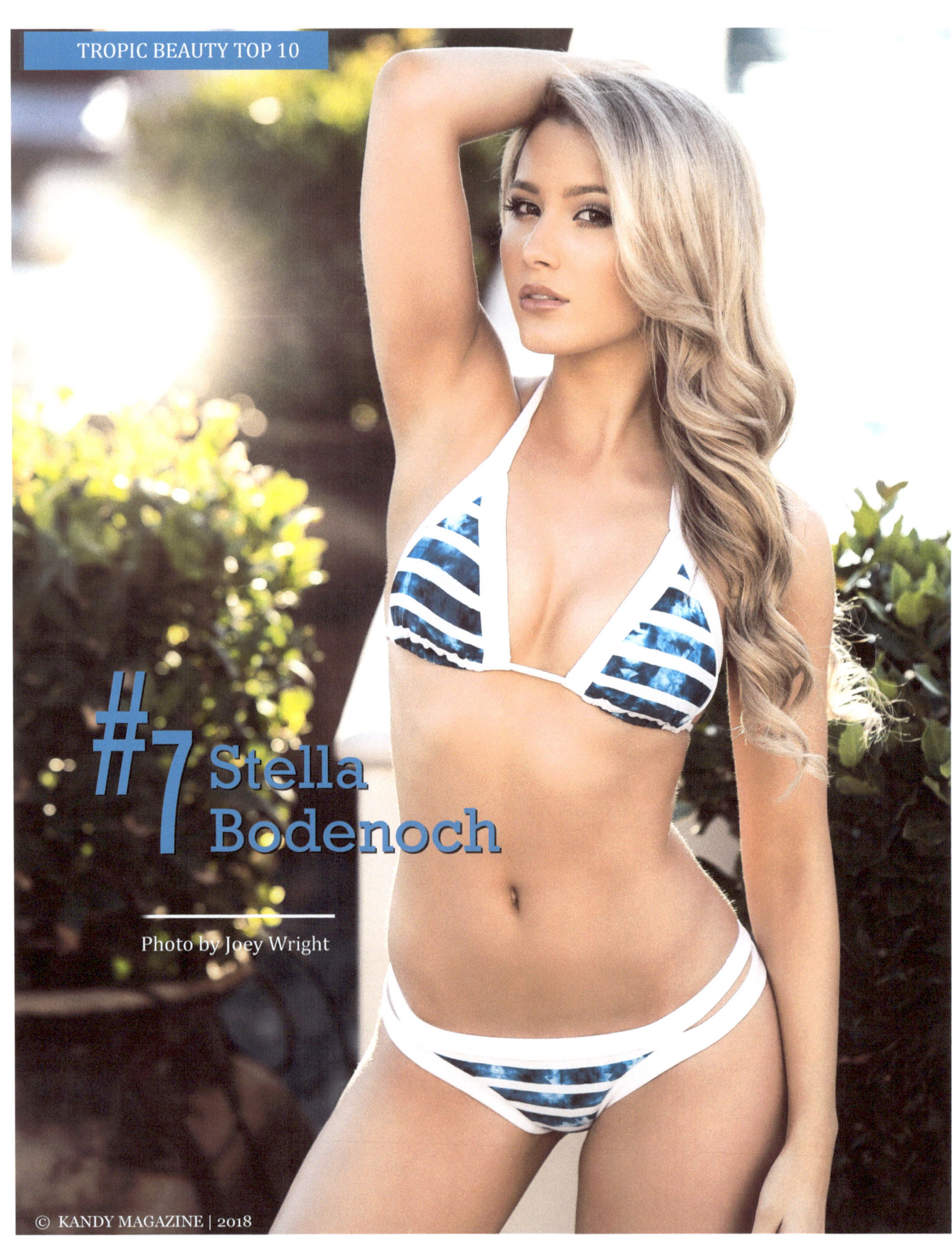

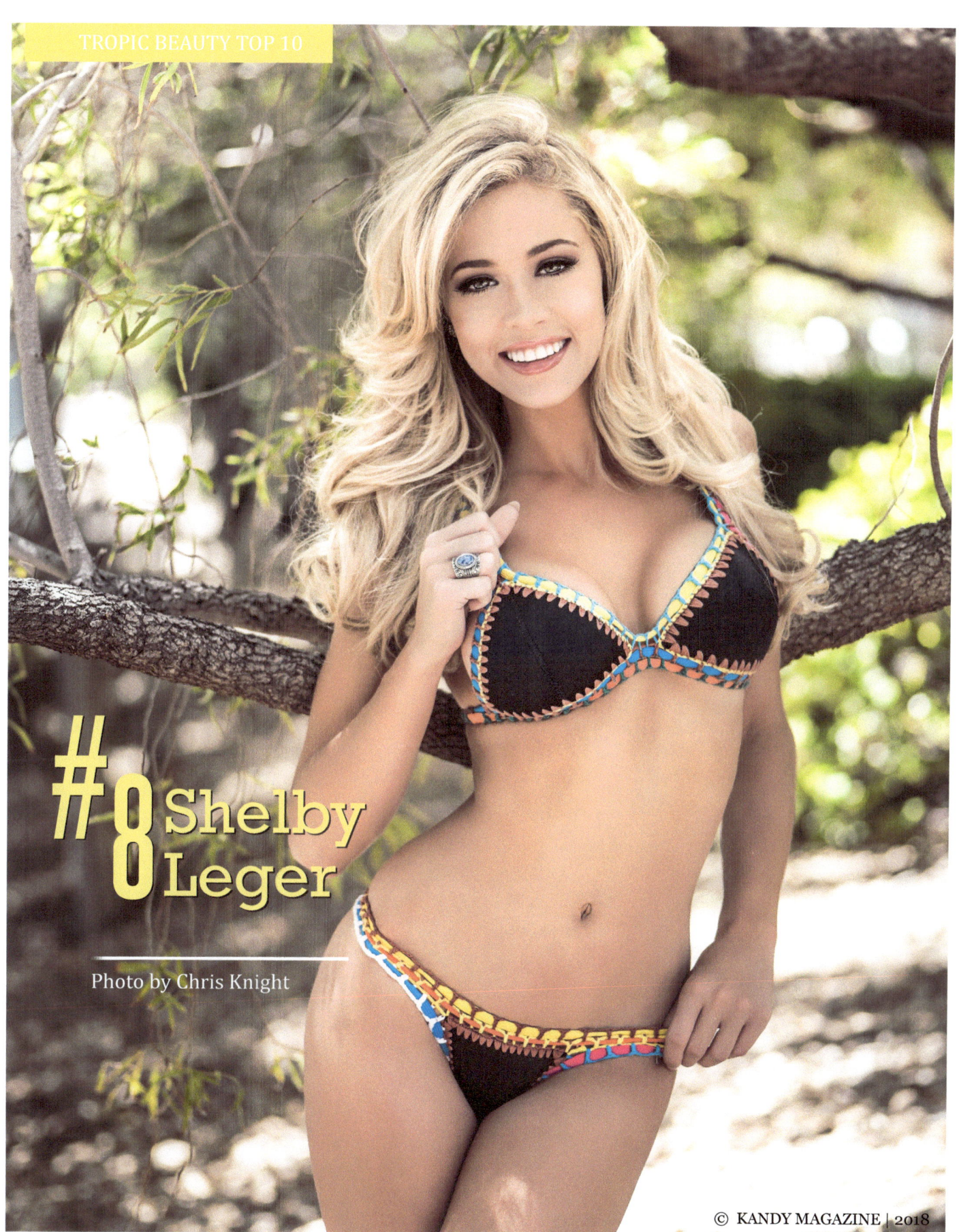

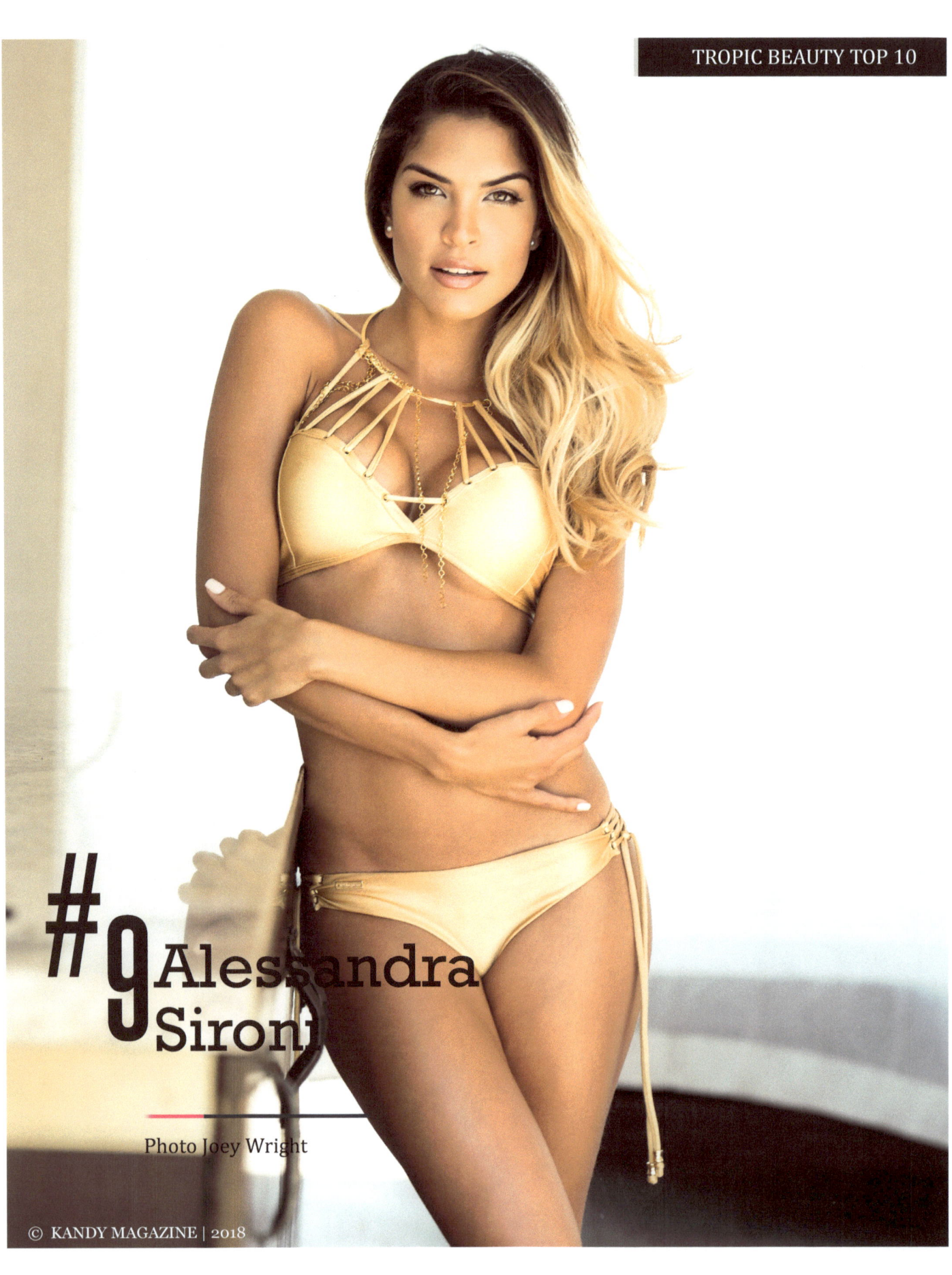

TROPIC BEAUTY TOP 10

#10 Mariah Coogan

Photo by Nick Suarez

© KANDY MAGAZINE | 2018

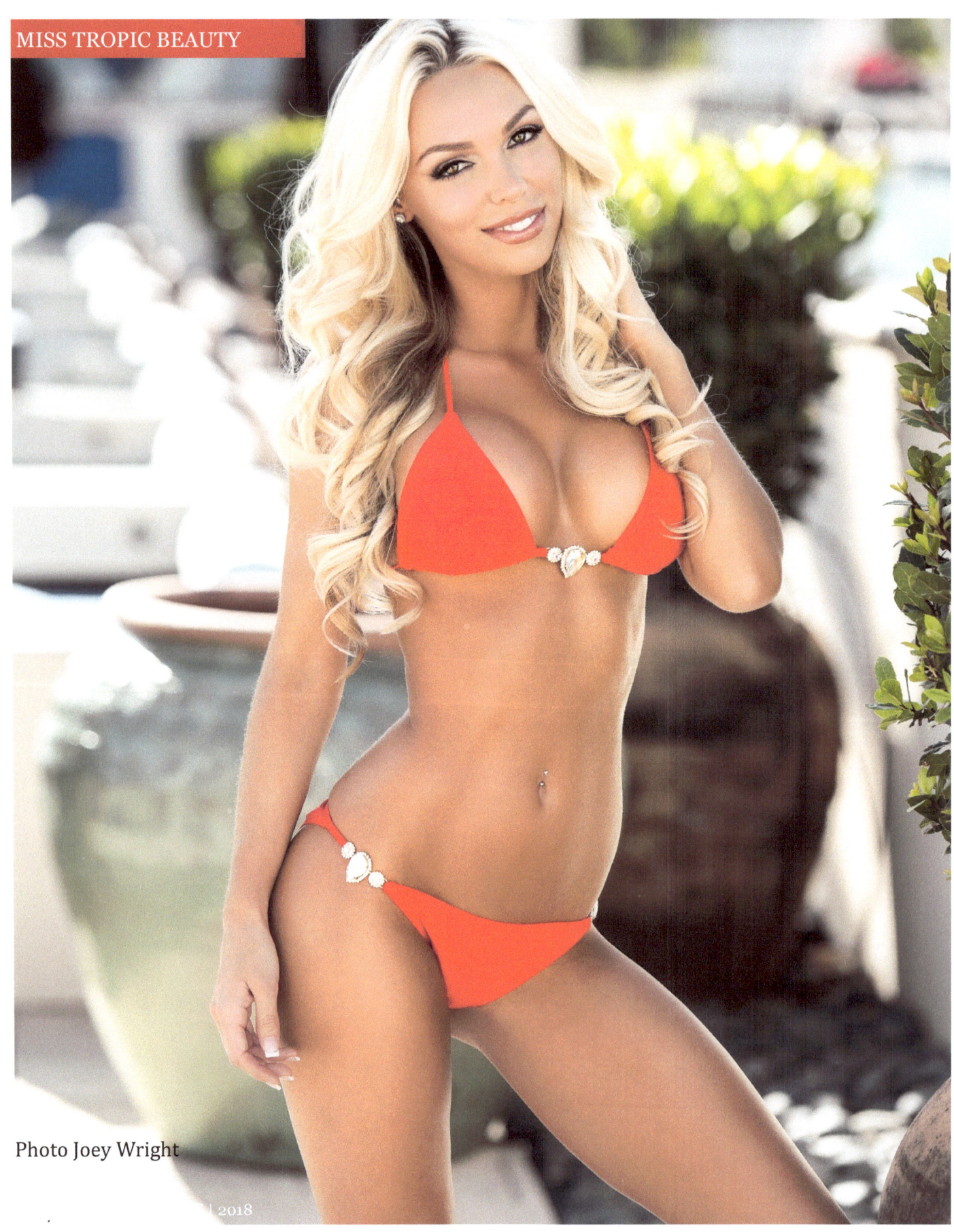

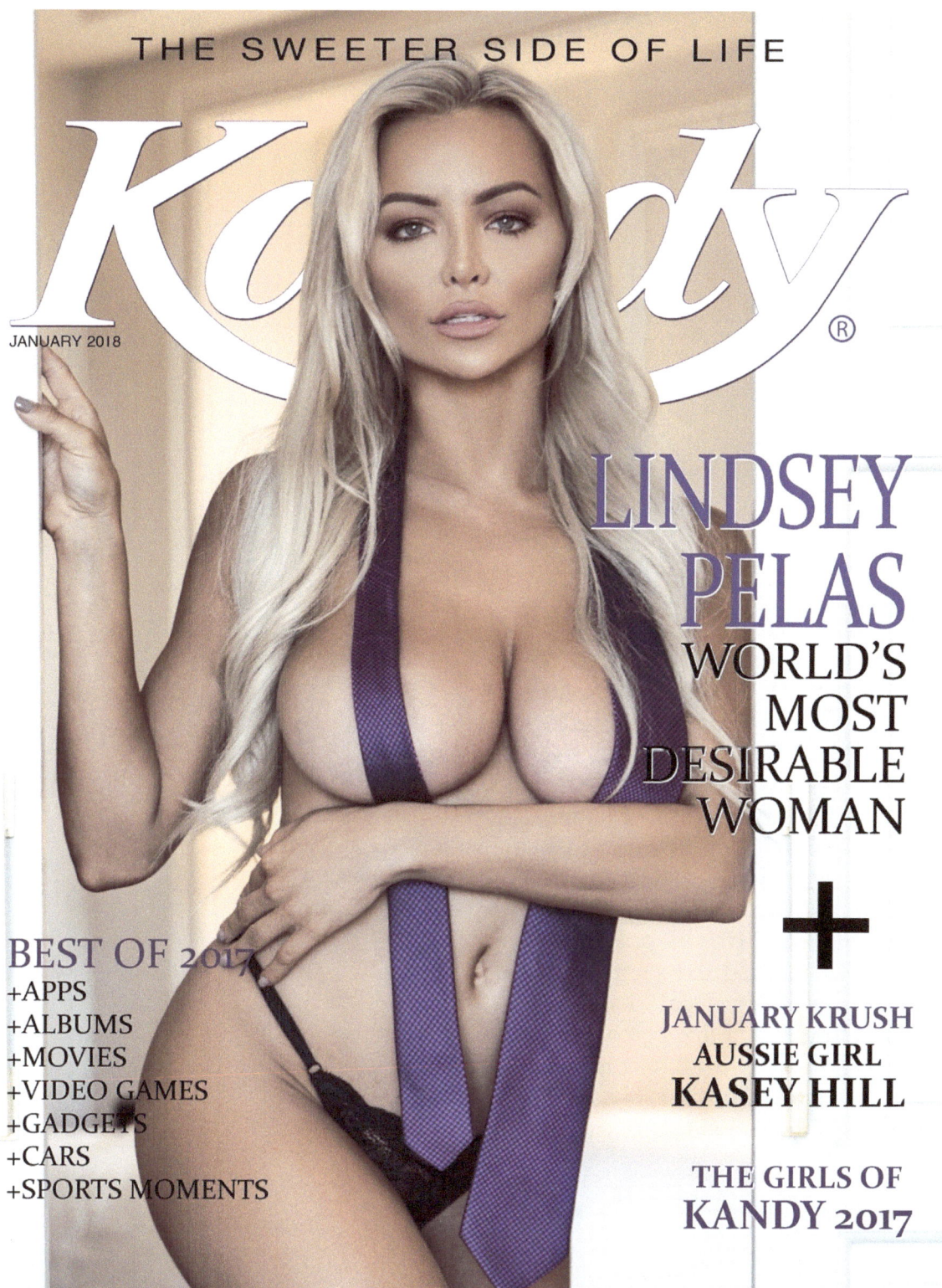

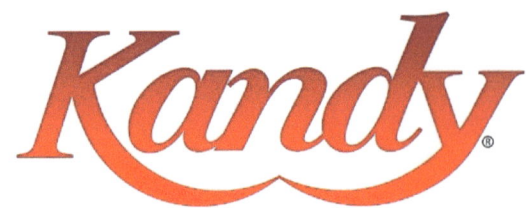

Editor in Chief
Ron Kuchler

Managing Editor
David Packo

Associate Editor
Steve Scala

Talent Director
Laurie Young

Marketing Director
Bill Nychay

Director of Photography
Mike Prado

Contributors
Joey Wright, Nick Suarez, Chris Knight, Tropic Beauty

Contact Us
Kandy Enterprises LLC
7260 W. Azure Dr Suite 140-639
Las Vegas, NV 89130
www.kandymag.com
facebook.com/kandymagazine
twitter.com/mykandymagazine
instagram.com/kandymag

General Inquiries - info@kandymag.com
Public Relations - pr@kandymag.com
Letters to The Editor - letters@kandymag.com
Copyright - legal@kandymag.com
Model Inquiries - kandymag.com/become-a-kandy-girl
Photographer Inquiries - kandymag.com/helpout
Writer Inquiries - kandymag.com/helpout
Subscription Inquiries - subscriptions@kandymag.com

Kandy Magazine
© 2018 Kandy Enterprises LLC. All Rights Reserved.

INSIDE

FRONT & BACK COVERS

INTENTIONALLY LEFT BLANK

---------- >

---------- >

www.ingramcontent.com/pod-product-compliance
Lightning Source LLC
Chambersburg PA
CBHW051836210526
45473CB00005B/1901